Ten Pre-Rapl

ex libris

Candlestick Press

Published by:
Candlestick Press,
Diversity House, 72 Nottingham Road,
Arnold, Nottingham NG5 6LF
www.candlestickpress.co.uk

Design, typesetting, print and production by Diversity Creative
Marketing Solutions Ltd., www.diversitymarketing.co.uk

Cover illustration: William Morris, Cartoon for stained glass, 1862
© Tate, London 2011
Introduction: © Ruth Robbins, 2011

ISBN 978 1 907598 06 7

Acknowledgements:
The publisher thanks Dr Ruth Robbins for her Introduction.

Introduction

In the politically-fraught 1840s – the so-called Hungry Forties –
artists and poets in England joined their counterparts elsewhere
in Europe and mounted their own (more muted) revolution in a
reaction against their predecessors. In a modest house in central
London in 1848, three young painters, Dante Gabriel Rossetti,
John Everett Millais and William Holman Hunt met to discuss the
future of pictorial and poetic art. With like-minded contemporaries
and friends, they cemented their views into an aesthetic
alliance against the staid conventions of academic painting in a
'Brotherhood' (though its circle included a number of women,
including Christina Rossetti) which they named the Pre-Raphaelite
Brotherhood. The title Pre-Raphaelite was – rightly or wrongly
– intended to signal a return to a purer past before the period of
Raphael, a period in which the symbolism of the medieval period
would be closely aligned to a realist technique that was often
almost photographic in its verisimilitude.

Not only were many paintings 'literary' – narrative in genre, and
drawing on poets such as Keats, Tennyson and Shakespeare – the
Pre-Raphaelites also wrote poems themselves. As is evident in
this pamphlet, all the poets use conventional forms – sonnets,
ballads, regular lyrics – to highly unconventional effect, often
focusing on emotions in a manner unfamiliar to Victorian
readers. 'My heart is like a singing bird,' declares Christina
Rossetti's poetic persona, for instance, and her poems are often
expressions of intense, though also 'innocent', emotions – joy,
happiness, love. The male poets went further, insisting in their
verses on powerful, often eroticized feelings. For example,
Algernon Charles Swinburne's 'Love and Sleep' offers an
explicit account of sexual love which glories in the beloved's
delectable body in a most un-Victorian way. These hungry young
men of the Hungry Forties and beyond show us their voracious
appetites at every turn of the page.

Dr Ruth Robbins

Silent Noon

Your hands lie open in the long fresh grass, –
The finger-points look through the rosy blooms:
Your eyes smile peace. The pasture gleams and glooms
'Neath billowing skies that scatter and amass.
All round our nest, far as the eye can pass,
Are golden kingcup-fields with silver edge
Where the cow-parsley skirts the hawthorn-hedge.
'Tis visible silence, still as the hour-glass.

Deep in the sun-searched growths the dragon-fly
Hangs like a blue thread loosened from the sky:-
So this wing'd hour is dropt to us from above.
Oh! clasp we to our hearts, for deathless dower,
This close-companioned inarticulate hour
When twofold silence was the song of love.

Dante Gabriel Rossetti (1828 - 1882)

The Cloud Confines

The day is dark and the night
To him that would search their heart;
No lips of cloud that will part
Nor morning song in the light:
Only, gazing alone,
To him wild shadows are shown,
Deep under deep unknown
And height above unknown height.
 Still we say as we go, –
"Strange to think by the way,
Whatever there is to know,
That shall we know one day."

The past is over and fled;
Named new, we name it the old;
Thereof some tale hath been told
But no word comes from the dead;
Whether at all they be,
Or whether as bond or free,
Or whether they too were we,
Or by what spell they have sped.
 Still we say as we go, –
"Strange to think by the way,
Whatever there is to know,
That shall we know one day."

What of the heart of hate
That beats in thy breast, O Time? –
Red strife from the furthest prime,
And anguish of fierce debate;
War that shatters her slain,
And peace that grinds them as grain,
And eyes fixed ever in vain
On the pitiless eyes of Fate.
 Still we say as we go, –
"Strange to think by the way,
Whatever there is to know,
That shall we know one day."

What of the heart of love
That bleeds in thy breast, O Man? –
Thy kisses snatched 'neath the ban
Of fangs that mock them above;
Thy bells prolonged unto knells,
Thy hope that a breath dispels,
Thy bitter forlorn farewells
And the empty echoes thereof?
Still we say as we go, –
"Strange to think by the way,
Whatever there is to know,
That shall we know one day."

The sky leans dumb on the sea,
Aweary with all its wings;
And oh! the song the sea sings
Is dark everlastingly.
Our past is clean forgot,
Our present is and is not,
Our future's a sealed seedplot,
And what betwixt them are we? –
We who say as we go, –
"Strange to think by the way,
Whatever there is to know,
That shall we know one day."

Dante Gabriel Rossetti (1828 - 1882)

The Hill Summit

This feast-day of the sun, his altar there
In the broad west has blazed for vesper-song;
And I have loitered in the vale too long
And gaze now a belated worshiper.
Yet may I not forget that I was 'ware,
So journeying, of his face at intervals
Transfigured where the fringed horizon falls, –
A fiery bush with coruscating hair.

And now that I have climbed and won this height,
I must tread downward through the sloping shade
And travel the bewildered tracks till night.
Yet for this hour I still may here be stayed
And see the gold air and the silver fade
And the last bird fly into the last light.

Dante Gabriel Rossetti (1828 - 1882)

Song

When I am dead, my dearest,
Sing no sad songs for me;
Plant thou no roses at my head,
Nor shady cypress tree:
Be the green grass above me
With showers and dewdrops wet;
And if thou wilt, remember,
And if thou wilt,
Forget.
I shall not see the shadow,
I shall not feel the rain;
I shall not hear the nightingale
Sing on, as if in pain:
And dreaming through the twilight
That doth not rise nor set,
Haply I may remember,
And haply may forget.

A Birthday

My heart is like a singing bird
Whose nest is in a watered shoot;
My heart is like an apple-tree
Whose boughs are bent with thick-set fruit;
My heart is like a rainbow shell
That paddles in a halcyon sea;
My heart is gladder than all these
Because my love is come to me.

Raise me a dais of silk and down;
Hang it with vair and purple dyes;
Carve it in doves, and pomegranates,
And peacocks with a hundred eyes;
Work it in gold and silver grapes,
In leaves, and silver fleurs-de-lys;
Because the birthday of my life
Is come, my love is come to me.

Christina Rossetti (1830 - 1894)

The First Spring Day

I wonder if the sap is stirring yet,
If wintry birds are dreaming of a mate,
If frozen snowdrops feel as yet the sun
And crocus fires are kindling one by one:
Sing, robin, sing;
I still am sore in doubt concerning Spring.

I wonder if the springtide of this year
Will bring another Spring both lost and dear;
If heart and spirit will find out their Spring,
Or if the world alone will bud and sing:
Sing, hope, to me;
Sweet notes, my hope, soft notes for memory.

The sap will surely quicken soon or late,
The tardiest bird will twitter to a mate;
So Spring must dawn again with warmth and bloom,
Or in this world, or in the world to come:
Sing, voice of Spring,
Till I too blossom and rejoice and sing.

Christina Rossetti (1830 - 1894)

Remember

Remember me when I am gone away,
Gone far away into the silent land;
When you can no more hold me by the hand,
Nor I half turn to go yet turning stay.
Remember me when no more day by day
You tell me of our future that you planned:
Only remember me; you understand
It will be late to counsel then or pray.
Yet if you should forget me for a while
And afterwards remember, do not grieve:
For if the darkness and corruption leaves
A vestige of the thoughts that once I had,
Better by far you should forget and smile
Than that you should remember and be sad.

Christina Rossetti (1830 - 1894)

The Message of the March Wind

Fair now is the spring-tide, now earth lies beholding
With the eyes of a lover, the face of the sun;
Long lasteth the daylight, and hope is enfolding
The green-growing acres with increase begun.

Now sweet, sweet it is thro' the land to be straying,
'Mid the birds and the blossoms and the beasts of the field;
Love mingles with love, and no evil is weighing
On thy heart or mine, where all sorrow is heal'd.

From township to township, o'er down and by tillage,
Far, far have we wander'd and long was the day;
But now cometh eve at the end of the village,
Where over the grey wall the church riseth grey.

There is wind in the twilight; in the white road before us
The straw from the ox-yard is blowing about;
The moon's rim is rising, a star glitters o'er us,
And the vane on the spire-top is swinging in doubt.

Down there dips the highway, toward the bridge crossing over
The brook that runs on to the Thames and the sea.
Draw closer, my sweet, we are lover and lover;
This eve art thou given to gladness and me.

Shall we be glad always? Come closer and hearken:
Three fields further on, as they told me down there,
When the young moon has set, if the March sky should darken,
We might see from the hill-top the great city's glare.

Hark, the wind in the elm-boughs! from London it bloweth,
And telleth of gold, and of hope and unrest;
Of power that helps not; of wisdom that knoweth,
But teacheth not aught of the worst and the best.

Of the rich men it telleth, and strange is the story
How they have and they hanker, and grip far and wide;
And they live and they die, and the earth and its glory
Has been but a burden they scarce might abide.

Hark! the March wind again of a people is telling;
Of the life that they live there, so haggard and grim,
That if we and our love amidst them had been dwelling,
My fondness had falter'd, thy beauty grown dim.

This land we have loved in our love and our leisure,
For them hangs in heaven, high out of their reach;
The wide hills o'er the sea-plain for them have no pleasure,
The grey homes of their fathers no story to teach.

The singers have sung and the builders have builded,
The painters have fashioned their tales of delight;
For what and for whom hath the world's book been gilded,
When all is for these but the blackness of night?

How long, and for what is their patience abiding?
How long and how oft shall their story be told,
While the hope that none seeketh in darkness is hiding
And in grief and in sorrow the world growth old?

Come back to the inn, love, and the lights and the fire,
And the fiddler's old tune and the shuffling of feet;
For there in a while shall be rest and desire,
And there shall the morrow's uprising be sweet.

Yet, love, as we wend, the wind bloweth behind us,
And beareth the last tale it telleth tonight,
How here in the spring-tide the message shall find us;
For the hope that none seeketh is coming to light.

Like the seed of midwinter, unheeded, unperish'd,
Like the autumn-sown wheat, 'neath the snow lying green,
Like the love that o'ertook us, unawares and uncherish'd,
Like the babe 'neath thy girdle that groweth unseen;

So the hope of the people now buddeth and groweth,
Rest fadeth before it, and blindness and fear;
It biddeth us learn all the wisdom it knoweth;
It hath found us and held us, and biddeth us hear:

For it beareth the message: 'Rise up on the morrow,
And go on thy ways toward the doubt and the strife;
Join hope to our hope and blend sorrow with sorrow,
And seek for men's love in the short days of life.'

But lo, the old inn, and the lights, and the fire,
And the fiddler's old tune and the shuffling of feet;
Soon for us shall be quiet and rest and desire,
And tomorrow's uprising to deeds shall be sweet.

William Morris (1834 - 1896)

Summer Dawn

Pray but one prayer for me 'twixt thy closed lips,
Think but one thought of me up in the stars.
The summer night waneth, the morning light slips,
Faint and grey 'twixt the leaves of the aspen,
                                    betwixt the cloud-bars,
That are patiently waiting there for the dawn:
Patient and colourless, though Heaven's gold
Waits to float through them along with the sun.
Far out in the meadows, above the young corn,
The heavy elms wait, and restless and cold,
The uneasy wind rises; the roses are dun;
Through the long twilight they pray for the dawn,
Round the lone house in the midst of the corn.
Speak but one word to me over the corn,
Over the tender, bow'd locks of the corn.

William Morris (1834 - 1896)

Love and Sleep

Lying asleep between the strokes of night
I saw my love lean over my sad bed,
Pale as the duskiest lily's leaf or head,
Smooth-skinned and dark, with bare throat made to bite,
Too wan for blushing and too warm for white,
But perfect-coloured without white or red.
And her lips opened amorously, and said –
I wist not what, saving one word – Delight.
And all her face was honey to my mouth,
And all her body pasture to mine eyes;
The long lithe arms and hotter hands than fire,
The quivering flanks, hair smelling of the south,
The bright light feet, the splendid supple thighs
And glittering eyelids of my soul's desire.

Algernon Charles Swinburne (1837 - 1909)